Having spent 10 years living close to nature ̶ ̶ ̶ ̶ ̶ ̶ ̶ ̶ ̶ ̶ ̶ ̶ ̶ ̶ ̶ Liz Mitten Ryan has co-authored four books describing a state of enlightened connection attained through this experience. *Sabbatical—Resting in the Miraculous Power of Isness* describes the universal journey to discover life's truth and higher meaning. It will lead you along a pathway to your true and immortal self.

Many spiritual teachers tell us that living in the present moment is the secret path to enlightenment. If we can let go of the past, the future, and time itself—still our busy minds, then the ego will be forgotten and in that brief instant we connect with God.

The biggest secret in this method is when thought ceases, quiet remains and in that quiet we let go of our physical identification and allow our spiritual truth to resonate within us. This truth is our heritage, it is from whence we came and to where we will return. In between we glimpse a memory of it in rare moments of selflessness; rare moments of reconnection with our higher selves and in turn God. When we touch God we experience Isness.

"Isness" is the glorious state of God manifested in his entire creative splendor here and on all planes. It is the active form of being, more a becoming, an awakening journey carrying one towards the adventure of vibrant aliveness, L.I.F.E (Love In Finite Expression) forever.

BIOGRAPHY

Liz Mitten Ryan has dedicated her life to understanding, communicating with, and helping animals. Over the past three years Liz has co-authored four award winning books with her dogs, cats and horses. Her art and her writing are strongly spiritual. *"It is in nature that I find life's answers. It is there, that one can interface with the wisdom and truth behind all creation; a vast ocean of information that nourishes all who bathe in it."* Liz has managed to touch many with her vision and her work has been presented to dignitaries throughout the world.

Liz is re-launching her web site www.lizmittenryan.com. The site now has a media section complete with radio and television interviews and videos showcasing the amazing level of connection between Liz and her horses, dogs, cats and Tesoro the steer (who will change your mind on eating meat!). The site also has a store where all four books will be available as print on demand through Amazon's BookSurge and many of the art images are available in a complete product line (everything from prints to tote bags) from Café Press. Liz's first book *One With the Herd* has won five independent publisher awards at Book Expo America and her art has raised millions of dollars for conservation groups and charities worldwide.

Liz also has a blog available on her web site where you can interact with Liz and the Herd and get up-to-date information on the happenings at Gateway 2 Ranch.

The website can also be accessed through the book titles at www.onewiththeherd.com, www.truthaccordingtohorses.com, www.lifeunbridled.com and www.sabbatical.com

www.lizmittenryan.com   www.sabbatical.com

Photographs by: Liz Mitten Ryan, Kevin Ryan, Laurie C. Munsell, and Nicole Reynolds.
Photo-graphics: Peter Ryan

Published and promoted by

Prima Publishing
250-377-3884

ISBN: 1-4392-1193-0

Printed in: USA

First Printing 2008

Liz Mitten Ryan

Prima Publishing
2008

To God,

In all his miraculous glory,
To whom I dedicate my life in all its possibility,
and my eternal and immeasurable LOVE.

Contents

Introduction

I have read many spiritual, metaphysical and new age books and understood and believed in the principles. What I haven't understood is why they are limited to human concepts and beliefs. Having spent a considerable time (ten years now) in the company of my animals and nature, I have absorbed a different perspective that is all encompassing in it's parameters. If one were to imagine a world very much like the original Garden of Eden state where all the creatures, animals, man and all of creation walked and talked with each other and God, it would be similar to the animals understanding when they connect to higher consciousness. From there, the force of love permeates all of life. There are no opposites, no death, only life everlasting. All experience is enjoyed through the power of the imagination and there is no possibility of harming another to obtain your desires. Removed from physical constraints, there would be no need for work or war to obtain assets that were always available. We would not need to kill. Life would be a sabbatical.

This vision comes from a higher plane of existence, both before and beyond our immersion in matter, a place where we can visit in our consciousness whenever we can leave the boundaries of our physical self. When we are not confined to a single identity we are free to travel wherever our consciousness would like to go.

That is true wisdom, truth, joy, freedom, abundance and love. That is who we truly are: UNLIMITED MIRACULOUS BEINGS—resting in the power of Isness. All of us one, in the creative genius of the Universe, the imagination of the All.

PEACE
by Kevin Ryan

In those quiet moments
When the soul
Takes a deep breath
And the air falls still
The senses soften
And an alertness of life's
Ebbing forces
Lifts the heart.

In those moments lies my peace
When our mountains dissolve
And fear's bitter taste
Tastes love's sweet freedom.
Life's purpose harmonizes
In those eternal moments
of joy.

In the beginning

"Isness" is the glorious state of God manifested in his entire creative splendor here and on all planes. It is the active form of being, more of a becoming—an awakened journey carrying one toward the adventure of vibrant aliveness, L.I.F.E (Love In Finite Expression) forever.

Isness is an extension to being . . . being in the ALL, the animals term for God as opposed to being in the now.

Isness just is—it exists for all time, in all dimensions. It is not a brief interlude, a now experience, but a knowing and becoming—a fluent state of wisdom and grace that embodies all creation.

Many spiritual teachers tell us that living in the present moment is the secret path to enlightenment. If we can let go of the past, the future, and time itself, and still our busy minds, then the ego will be forgotten, and in that brief instant we will connect with God.

The biggest secret in this method is when thought ceases, quiet remains, and in that quiet, we let go of our physical identification and allow our spiritual truth to resonate within us. This truth is our heritage. It is from whence we came and to where we will return. In between we glimpse a memory of it in rare moments of selflessness—rare moments of reconnection with our higher selves, and, in turn, God.

The horses said it beautifully in my earlier book, *The Truth According to Horses*. When asked the question "Can you give us a simple definition of what you call religion? I'm sure it differs greatly from what we believe," the herd replied:

> Religion is to us a certitude, not a belief; not an indoctrination; not a confine, but an absolute; a knowing and a truth that is given the moment we connect to the ALL (God). It needs no doctrine, no rules; it is absolutely remembered as the fabric of all life, an understanding that is our first and last breath and everything relevant in between.

I have begun to know a whole new reality through connection to animals. They live in a place devoid of ego, past, future, and time. This does not imply a state of inaction where one must lie about in a meditative state, blissing in that connection. Going back to the word "Isness" again: My cat Ben—Min Buddha Ben Puss Ha, a true contemplative—gave me that word. He sent me the thought "Isness is my business," and it was certainly true. A big white Buddha, Ben purred his way through life, never making a sound; he would just open his mouth to transmit a message and nothing would come out. True silence. In the end, when we had to have him put down, the vet said in disbelief, "I have never seen a cat purr his way through euthanasia." A true spiritual master, he was not dependent on circumstance for his bliss.

I have learned from my animals another secret path to enlightenment. It involves simply living in a quiet, natural state, as does all of creation except humans. Very much like rocking a baby to sleep, the peaceful lull of the natural world is hypnotic. In our original state, before our fall from grace, we lived as the animals do. We absorbed and communed with our surroundings. In this state of communion, there was no separateness, no barriers; we were one with all life and God, or the ALL, which is all life.

> I think the key is in the sabbatical. Our lives have become so goal-oriented. We feel that we must constantly achieve, and the more the better.

Living here in the quiet, surrounded by the natural world, I am somehow allowed to slip back to that state. Barriers dissolve and my sense of self diminishes until I am at once lost and yet found in the congregation of spirit.

Once one has experienced a moment when self fades, its boundaries melding with the larger Self, which is God (ALL), there is no going back. We have experienced the knowing that passeth all understanding. "He who hath seen me has seen the Father." In that moment, all knowledge, all understanding is given, and we are forever changed. We remember; the Christ within us is born, and that star will forever after shine in our hearts. "Amazing Grace," it has been called, but words cannot describe a state where words are meaningless, diminished in the infinite knowing that makes words unnecessary.

Here in this state, all is given. There is no definition, and language, species, color, and creed are all forgotten—drops of water in the same ocean.

As my horses said in *Life Unbridled: What Animals Have to Teach Us about Spiritual Freedom*:

Imagine living with the perspective of being inside and outside of yourself at the same time, as we do. We can experience all aspects of life on this plane and beyond—the greater ALL existence. The moment you make that connection, everything is given. It is like a drop of water becoming the ocean, a beam of light blending with all light. Within and without there is nothing else—we become all form itself, Oneness—ALL.

The moment we touch the ALL, we become the ALL. It is a joy and a homecoming that is immeasurable. This is what we have to teach you about spiritual freedom. Do not imagine yourself as a drop of water or a beam of light when you are the ocean and the sky. Do not imagine yourself to be the world when you are the universe. You have nothing to fear but fear itself. Fear is a finite piece of freedom, and freedom is all there is. As a drop of rain falls into the ocean and evaporates again to become a cloud, such is your life. Let us help you gain a new perspective.

In six days God created the heavens and the earth, and on the seventh day he rested. This is the model God created for us to follow as fully actualized spiritual beings co-creating with him on the earth or physical plane. Actually he co-creates through us when we invite Christ, or God manifest, into our lives. It is no longer the little "i" but the big "I" manifesting the individual and unique personal skills of each individual to create on the physical plane. God, being Spirit, can only exist on the physical plane through us. The Sabbath day—or Sabbatical—is the time we must spend "resting in the now," as Ekhardt says, meditating and connecting to God. Then we must go out into the world and

co-create with God, armed with that peace, understanding, and connection that we have obtained. If we were all to sit around in the Now all week, then what would God accomplish—how would we evolve?

This is Isness as opposed to "Being"—Being in the ALL as opposed to being in the Now. As unlimited God-beings, or more accurately, God-*becomings*, we have the creative freedom to travel anywhere we desire in the ALL, within God's creation—past, present, or future—anytime, on any plane! We must not dwell in the moment of the Now, but get on with God's work and then rest and reconnect in his presence. As we become truly adept at this communion, then we can carry God's presence with us, *around* us as the cloak of Christ, everywhere we go.

Horses are true masters of Isness. Being in their presence requires our focus on the moment and connection to our own unique truth within the framework of the greater truth of life.

I think the key is in the sabbatical. Our lives have become so goal-oriented. We feel that we must constantly achieve, and the more the better. We have sold ourselves into slavery for want of a bigger house and a better car. When we get them, our lives are still empty. Why? Because the only thing that can make us truly happy is connection—connection is the wellspring from which flows all that we don't even know is our heart's desire, until it comes to us via that one link that is our lifeline to spirit.

We will never, ever be happy fulfilling our own desires because we are so estranged from our authentic selves that we don't even know what they are. If we achieve fame and fortune at the cost of the only true love we will ever know, it is empty and we are empty. That love is our essence, our true selves, and it is the root of all our desires. Until we find it, we are empty and desolate, and we look everywhere, trying to relieve the pain of our emptiness. How can we find it?

We must take time from our busy lives to rest in the quiet. As Premiere Edition (Prima) says, speaking for the herd, "You forget yourself in nature, in quiet (the true quiet void of thoughts), and you remember a truth you knew long ago that has drowned in the confusion of your busy life."

We can, of course, do yoga, meditation, tai chi, while sitting in a sterile and unnatural environment, or more simply, we can reconnect with our roots in the garden of our choice. We can walk and talk with the natural world. Our connection becomes more profound if we are in the presence of large spirits like rocks and trees and animals—particularly animals, for they are our simpler cousins. Animals never left the Garden, and so they hold for us the picture of life at the level of absolute truth. Because they have not slipped into an ego state, animals share with us their vision. Like children, they cannot be anything but truthful. They have not learned to deceive.

My horses have defined (equine) truth as "absolute Truth from its inception at the thought level, to its reverberation in every fiber of the being." Horses are true masters of Isness. Being in their presence requires our focus on the moment and connection to our own unique truth within the framework of the greater truth of life.

Lying to a horse has huge consequences, as anyone who has ever tried to pretend around them will tell you. They expose you in a moment! They enjoy it. Many a time Prima has called my

bluff and made me look like an absolute fool. She is training me to be truthful from my thoughts to my body language.

Animals are saints. They are great spiritual teachers because they are absolutely honest and they have not lost their connection to the ALL. Humans have lost their instincts and with them, their intuition. They are powdered and perfumed, buried under a veneer of plastic perfection. Why would anyone want to be a mannequin—a Barbie or a Ken doll with all its parts smoothed into a facade of posed perfection, their connection to the flow a ride along the conveyer belt of mass production? This is what most of humanity—at least, those who have the affluence to reflect upon their desires—aspire to be: like their neighbors, but better, more plastic and perfect. Detached from their longing, they find themselves lost in the labyrinth, lost in a hall of mirrors reflecting only the plastic perfection of their veneer.

From Magical Edition, speaking for the horses:

I would like to speak of fidelity. Fidelity is more powerful even than truth, and is the largest aspect that horses bring forth. Each created thing has a unique and special facet of its own particular expression that is a vibrational blueprint in constant formulation. Much like a tuning fork, each species is held in orchestra, in a particular similar vibration by a conductor responsible for that piece of music. You have heard of high-fidelity sound, and that is what a species in perfect tune represents. As members of an orchestra must follow the conductor, tune their instruments, and study the music if they are to create a symphony of the purest, highest fidelity, so must each created form and species strive to maintain the purity of vibration, unique not only to their individual and larger incarnation, but as well to their spiritual form, both individual and larger and again larger still, so as to encompass the concert of life itself.

This requires a purity of intent, of lifestyle, and a clarity achieved only in the silent moments of meditative experience. All life forms except for man—plants, minerals, animals—achieve this balance of individual truth within the greater truth of life by opening to the music of the spheres and allowing each individual vibration to tune and influence their own. When we are open and responsive to the spiritual and physical energies, our life opens like a flower in response to the sun and the gifts of the earth.

People have long forgotten how to feel the earth between their toes and breathe the energy through their skin. They have lost the music that is blocked by the noise of their endeavor. They are looking so hard for something they have had all along, and the further they search, the harder it is to find. They must seek silence to hear the sound.

Time spent in our company will tune and strengthen that forgotten connection. We are large and strong in our vibration. Spend time in our midst and we will lead you toward fidelity, as an individual, a species, and a fully integrated spiritual creation.

It is time. It is necessary to reconnect with our heritage and our true home. We need to pull ourselves away from the bright lights and the circuitry, long enough to discover what is truly important, what is truly meaningful, and what is the only thing we can have forever—our true selves.

Possibility

We as humans suffer from an insidious malaise that is growing like a cancer throughout our species and our world. Natural System Dysfunction (NSD) is a direct result of our alienation from our natural, life-giving relationship to our source—the source of all creation and the sustenance that feeds all life. The more we distance ourselves from our natural state, the more dangerous and fragile our tenuous hold on life becomes.

To avoid sounding as unintelligent as the average human being who says "Speak louder, I don't understand your language," the solution to NSD lies in our ability to listen to the language of nature—a language beyond words. It speaks softly, but with wisdom, instantly remembered as absolute truth, both for the individual and for the whole as one united symbiotic system and greater being. This is what the animals call the ALL (God).

I don't think you will find an animal with NSD unless it has somehow been made so by a human, i.e., held in captivity under forced and unnatural circumstances.

The human antidote to NSD currently being developed is the science of organic psychology, which enables your thinking and feeling to consciously work *with* rather than against nature. In other words, you need to return to your roots as an organic design, subject to the organic laws of nature, but rather than consciously working with nature, we can, in fact, *play* with it and allow nature to play with us. Isness is the fastest route. It transports us instantly to connect with the ALL and benefit from the immensity and wisdom of an infinite resource, and our truth as spiritual beings temporarily immersed in matter.

> **True connection can only be discovered in the absence of thought, and going about simple tasks in the presence of nature and animals is the fastest route to that state.**

How can we fully appreciate the possibility of Isness? We must reconnect to our source. Although this can be done from a meditative state, found by removing ourselves from the distractions of our unnatural lives, it is difficult and time-consuming to attain this state by sheer will. The secret of continuous and facile meditation, or as the Hindu Buddhists call it, active *Samadhi*, is connection to all life. Samadhi describes a non-dualistic state of consciousness in which the consciousness of the experiencing subject becomes one with the experienced object. True connection can only be discovered in the absence of thought, and going about simple tasks in the presence of nature and animals is the fastest route to that state. As my horses tell me:

> Our lives are one continuous conversation with God, or the ALL. We recognize that when humans converse with God, it becomes a revelation. But why must humans take ownership of everything? Your translation voices a collective ownership of God within all humans. God is

within all life! We are no less because we speak a different language, or because our skin or our culture is foreign. We have much to teach humanity about the ALL. All life is symbiotic. Do not forget us. The part about dominion is only written in human religions.

You humans speak much of enlightenment. What is enlightenment? We suppose, for humans, it is that ever-evasive lightness of being. It is difficult for you; you struggle to achieve; you struggle to avoid; you just plain *struggle*, when the true secret of enlightenment is to simply "be in the light," to "be of the light." You humans are "of the dark" most of the time. You enjoy the stimulation of game playing, which to us is simply untruth. We are honest, absolute; you will not find an animal pretending to be anything other than their God-given selves.

It is strange how your truisms speak the truth, but you rarely hear them. You are mostly too busy to listen. That is the secret: You must listen, and to listen you must be quiet; you must quiet your minds.

What we know of you is confusing—a tangled jumble of thoughts and desires. One moment you think and feel one way; the next moment, another. Horses have a hard time with this because our minds are like a clear pool. We are the waters of the earth and we reflect the sky. We do not claim ownership of the waters, but share them with all who would come to drink. We have not forgotten the truth of who we are. We are the water and the sky. We are the magic of light in form, and light cannot be held captive but for a moment in time. And then there is no time except when we try to steal a finite piece of the ALL and hold it captive for our own appreciation. A sparkle in a drop of dew here, now, only for an instant—immortal only in the memory of the ALL.

There is only one possibility for your recovery. You must give up ownership; you must give up desire to have anything for yourselves alone. If we can "pray for our recovery," as Thomas Merton says, then, God willing, our will should become his will for us, a free flow of light through life—through our individual lives, wonderful and unique, in every way a facet of the ALL, as necessary to life as life itself. We are, each and every one of us, created beings, one with life itself; we are as necessary to the course of creation as the blood that flows through our veins is to our very being. If, in fact, we could surrender to the life force and trust in the wisdom that directs the individual flow of blood in all life, then we could be as carefree as that flow of blood, of tides, of seasons, and of life itself.

What are we, the created ones, but a mound of dust—a lifeless mound of dust, without the breath of spirit to give us wings. I have always felt from a very young age that my wings were something I must earn—a badge of merit that required a lot of learning to reclaim.

I do remember figuratively putting up my hand when asked, "Who will volunteer for God?" I will, I said, not even faintly understanding the assignment. But I would do it again and again. I would do it forever, because when one truly loves God and understands that there really is nothing beyond or before that state of absolute belonging, then there is nothing else that matters.

The problem is that when we come to the earth plane, we are plunged into matter from spirit—earth dust from

stardust—and we are in the dark. The light is far away, a distant memory that grows ever dimmer with immersion into mass mind. The only way to maintain the connection is to commune with the natural world and maintain an open relationship with earth and animal energy.

In reality, our wings are our birthright; we do not have to earn them, but we do have to remember to look after them. We are born to the possibility of achieving Christhood—the possibility of becoming a clear conduit of God, manifest in matter.

I remember years ago being given a picture of God (and I think the animals' term, the ALL, says it better). God was pictured as an enormous light made up of smaller, intricate, and multifaceted lights, or light bodies, each attached to earth bodies, so that, in fact, we are all the ALL. The clarity and strength of our connection shines through our earth bodies, each unique form or earth body brilliant in its connection to the ALL.

Christ, Muhammad, and Buddha were clear facets—prisms, if you will—through which the light of the ALL became the splendor of a rainbow, clearly conveying the myriad beauty of the God-being.

To even hope to attain that state of perfection within the confines of matter, we must keep our connection to our light bodies clean and open. We must bathe in the energy of other clear light bodies. The natural world is energized with light. The trees, rocks, water, and plants are all vibrant in their reflection of the ALL. It is in their presence that we can rest, absorb, and reflect the energy that so clearly emanates from the pure life force. When we experience the incredible beauty of nature in harmony—a sunset, a spring day, the majesty and myriad beauty of the changing days and seasons—we all know moments of *Satori*, a Zen Buddhist state of intuitive illumination.

> The clarity and strength of our connection shines through our earth bodies, each unique form or earth body brilliant in its connection to the ALL.

We remember and reconnect with our true selves, our one self, which is the ALL. When we experience that connection, the individual becomes for an instant again the whole, vibrating in symphony with the ALL. We are renewed, refreshed, and reawakened. When we return to the mass-mind confusion of the human experience, we are forever changed by the memory of magic.

In the Bible, the woman who wanted only to touch the robe of Christ symbolizes the fact that when we touch or are touched by spirit, we are forever changed. When we experience the quiet and healing of nature in the company of animals—and particularly, our companion animals: dogs, cats, and horses—then the illumination and rejuvenation is intensified.

From my cat, Ben:

It is interesting how you humans say one minute that God is within all life, but then you narrow that statement to, "We (meaning humans) are the image or essence of God." If God is within all life, then why would some of that life be more like God than others? Here, in spirit, it is all very clear that form is a temporary expression. My consciousness, which is a segment of the ALL, can express itself in any form I choose. I can experience a flower, a sunset, a cat, a fish, or a man. I am simply consciousness that takes shape according to my thoughts.

When I am experiencing different forms, my consciousness is still "I," and if you examine the semantics, everyone and everything identifies with "I." We are all "I," a point of consciousness, and we are all no different from each other as far as consciousness goes. Because I choose to manifest as a cat, it does not make me less worthy. We have, and will, experience all aspects of expression. The big difference with humans is that they have forgotten all this. When they separated from the ALL, they became self-absorbed and developed a belief system of their own. Their truth is not universal truth, and they have become blind and deaf to information that might contradict their beliefs. When you all believed the world was flat, it took many brave adventurers to dispel that myth. To go beyond the veil, at least when you are experiencing on the physical plane, you need our help.

Instead of cataloging us as lesser beings, entertain the possibility that we are just different. Explore what we offer, talk to us, spend time being open to our energy and the energy of nature. You will not find people who live in nature who are apart and separate from the rest of life. They communicate and share with all living things. When you do this, we will take you beyond the veil, for we have not forgotten the truth and isolated ourselves in a finite world of opposites. You, the supposed intelligent ones, have used that intelligence to invent your own world. You thought you could do better than the ALL, but you are beginning to see evidence of your error. You have repeated this pattern for all time, thinking that your country, race, religion, house, clothes, car, thoughts, are better than another's, and as a whole, your species is better than all other species. Don't you see where all of your competition has gotten you? There will always be someone to argue with you.

We animals do not compare. We go about our business of Isness. Being is all we experience, and we share that being with all creation. Let us take you to the place of truth, where there are no opposites or differences, a place where there is only spiritual freedom—beyond the veil.

Animals are clear conduits—they never lose their connection to the ALL, and they can show us the clear vision of their understanding. We absorb that wisdom by simply being quiet and open in their presence.

As Picasso, my two-year-old horse, wrote:

Let us explore
the possibility of our communion
together . . .
We contribute something new,
and as yet undiscovered
by us . . .
and life itself.

BUTTERFLY
by Kevin Ryan

Somewhere out of the early morning light, a movement stirred in the visage of tree, grass, and flower. Slowly, in arcing movements, jerking along a seemingly random pattern, the butterfly approached the awakening flower. Aroused by the fluttering silence and vibrant colors, a curiosity grew from stem to petal. "If only such beauty could alight upon me, touch me. Oh, what joy it would bring! What questions I would have, of rootless existence enlightened upon the breeze, free to travel unhindered as a child of the sun and wind." And so the flower dreamed as the butterfly coursed along the air currents.

"So here I am again upon my aimless quest of the landscape," the butterfly pondered. With its purpose fueled by the rays of the sun, it circled, searching for a companion.

The Wilderness Experience

We are all born into the wilderness experience. We come from a plane where all is light. In light, nothing can be hidden, nothing is separate and apart from its source and destination—it is Isness. Light is love, freedom, joy, wisdom, abundance, truth; it is unlimited—it is ALL. ALL is given, ALL is . . . We have no need to strive or struggle, no need to maintain a separate identity or try to acquire something that is ours alone. We are not alone. We are life itself, everlasting—we are all one.

When I first experienced this indescribable understanding, I was twenty-two years old. I had forayed into life's mysteries, always searching to grasp the faint memory of a knowing that just superseded my understanding. Now and again I would catch glimpses—almost like trying to remember dreams—and they would resonate somehow with the memory of light. Around the time that I had my first light experience, I was confused and saddened by the contrast of what I had seen of life, to what I knew in the deepest fiber of my being to be the truth.

I was lying on my bed, praying, asking God for the answers to life. Why were we here? What did he want us to accomplish? Suddenly the room faded and I was immersed in a vibration I experienced as a loud hum. I could feel myself rising, and although I was very tempted to hang on to my senses, the essence I was being drawn toward was so compelling that I wanted more than life itself to reunite with this force, which can only be described as *love*. It felt like I was going home to my mother, father, friends, relatives, and every moment where I had ever experienced love in any form. Yet it was more than that. It was also something that I remembered—a place, a part of me that was my home—my true self.

Around the time that I had my first light experience, I was confused and saddened by the contrast of what I had seen of life, to what I knew in the deepest fiber of my being to be the truth.

I have no idea how long I was bathed in the light. I was the ALL, and I was at once and for always illuminated. I remembered a truth that was everything that mattered: We are God-beings, God-becomings. We are ALL there is, ALL-ways. We have all volunteered for this mission, this plunge into darkness, and it is only our knowledge that light illuminates darkness and proves that it does not in fact exist, and our love, that allows us to take this leap.

This earth plane is the wildest wilderness. We are born into a heavy darkness and must begin to learn the laws that govern this strange and hostile world. The only familiar feeling is the warmth of our mother's breast, a comfort that we cling to in this alien environment. Over time we absorb and mimic our parents' grasp of physical laws, fettered as they are by mass-mind belief. It is only those of us that can maintain our connection to the light in the company of animals and nature that do not get drawn

deeply into the circuitry of the human computer program that we are all burdened with.

The horses explain their understanding, which remains clear to all animals because they do not identify with the human dream, which would cause them to lose their connection to the truth.

From Divine Edition, speaking for the herd—book 2

There is a dream that is held in the mind of God. It lives in the realms of spirit with all that ever was, or is, or will ever be. It just *is*. We live that dream; it is as much a part of who we are, or more so, than this life we share on earth.

There is a place, Man, where we live and dream together. And there was a time long past when we shared that memory here on earth. That truth is lost to you. You no longer see beyond the false constructs of your ego, and most of you have lost the vision of anything outside yourselves. The truth is, we are one; that dream is still alive, and all of those in the dream are waiting for you to join us.

Wake up, people! There is a golden rule in your Bible that says "Do unto others as you would have them do unto you." That is because we are all individual cells of one enormous spiritual being. These cells unite to form organs and systems, and all are interdependent in order to survive. The same thoughts and emotions travel throughout this being. Love that is held in its heart strengthens all of the organs and systems, and thoughts that are true and good benefit every cell. This being cannot survive without its lungs or its liver. All of these individual organs speak a different language; they have specific and important contributions to make for the life of the body, but they are all interconnected by the same intelligence, emotions, and wisdom. All of us will only be fully actualized, complete, spiritual beings when we know this truth and are united in understanding and in love—when we love our neighbors as ourselves because we are *one*.

We all know this truth on one level. It is repeated again and again in our books: "Do unto others . . . love thy neighbor as thyself . . . as you give, you shall receive . . . to thine own self be true, and it shall follow as the day follows night." We learn and then we forget; the truth and the light seem to get lost in the darkness. Christ's wilderness experience is symbolic for our earth journey. We are alone in the unknown, we do without all our comforts, we are tempted and tried, promised all the worldly possessions we could ever want if we turn away form our connection with God. The devil is simply our ego, our belief in separateness, our lacks and limitations—our belief that we are alone in the wilderness and subject to evil. Evil is like the darkness: It cannot exist in the presence of light. We are light beings; we are all that is, so evil exists only in the shadowy world of mass belief—the world of darkness inhabited by those who have lost their way to the light, and those who have forgotten who they really are.

In the Native American tradition, young initiates who are searching for spiritual truth go on a spirit quest. They go alone into nature to listen for the truth, and they find it in visions that become clear in the serenity of the natural world.

When I first moved to my wilderness (our secluded 320-acre ranch) and spent several months living in a wall tent, I was mostly alone. I spent my days in the company of my dogs, cat, and horses, roaming the land and absorbing the ever-changing beauty. I would spend hours watching the horses, being one with the herd and the land itself.

After a time I began to realize that concepts would spontaneously become available to my uncluttered mind. These concepts came from beyond me, it seemed, from a consciousness that was united in the understanding of truth—universal truth. When I would receive these ideas, it was somewhat like having a microchip implanted in my brain. I just knew everything instantly—no questions—and I knew it was the Truth. It took me a long time, and, in fact, I had almost finished writing my first book, *One With the Herd*, when I suddenly realized that I was not really writing the book . . . not in the true sense. Rather, it was simply given to me, one idea after another. I had no plan, no concepts, no knowledge of where it was going, or even where it was coming from. I would simply rest in that quiet state that I managed to be able to revisit again and again once I had unlocked the door. It was a vibration of oneness, and I could resonate with it at will. It was like resting in the power of Isness, a place I could go to rest and escape from the busyness of the created world.

It wasn't until I neared the end of writing this first book (one that I'd written to help horses and animals generally) that I thought to ask the horses for any thoughts or ideas they might

It was only humans who had lost this ability when they began to identify with their finite identity, the ego.

want to contribute. They wrote the dedication, the prologue, the epilogue, and supplied dozens of other quotes, and as I scribed their ideas, I began to realize that they came from the same place of understanding as had my other ideas. It suddenly became clear to me that this was Universal Mind. The horses were able to access this wisdom at all times. The lightbulb went on and glowed ever more brightly. By being part of nature and in the company of my animals, I had become tuned to their vibration. Our minds joined together with the greater, all-encompassing Universal Mind—or, as the horses were later to share with me, the ALL. It appeared that all animals—in fact, all living creatures—were clearly in communion with the ALL at all times. It was only humans who had lost this ability when they began to identify with their finite identity, the ego.

The more time I spent with my animals in the quiet of nature, the more easily and often I could rest in this place of knowing. I began to ask them questions, and I would only have to hold the picture of my herd in my mind's eye (visualizing each member individually but addressing them as a group) and the answers would be given to me. Sometimes in words, sometimes in pictures, and often in an instant transfer of knowledge, I would receive what I realized to be the truth. I began trying it with my dogs and cats, and again, the answers would come from that same place. This wisdom was available whenever I connected to my animals, even to those who had left the earth plane and were now in spirit. There seems to be no barriers to instant communication when minds are joined. There was no small talk or individualism, just oneness of being, all united in a common truth. The interesting

variant was that each individual cat, horse, or dog had their own unique interpretation of the truth.

Prima, my firstborn (horse-child), and biggest challenge and reward, had always been haughty and opinionated. Her personality resembled her interpretation of the truth. It was as if her mission was to illuminate mankind, and she was somewhat didactic, although wonderfully metaphorical in her prose. I found some of my animals eager to be heard from, while others were somewhat shy or disinterested. On the whole, it was as if they were saying "What took you so long to be open to communication and to speak and listen to us telepathically?" This is how all living creatures communicate, although humans, only occasionally.

In my third book, *Life Unbridled: What Animals Teach Us about Spiritual Freedom*, I was given the understanding that consciousness is ALL and ALL is consciousness. There is only one consciousness. When you realize the implications of this truth, you realize that thoughts anywhere in the world, human or animal, are all available to you.

> It is consciousness that is life and that exists forever—bodies come and go.
> —The Animals

> Animals interconnect, species to species to man, and that is how we can help you.
> —Premiere Edition (Prima), speaking for the herd

It is easy to lose connection to consciousness when one is self-absorbed. You have to be able to disengage from the incessant chatter of individual mind to be open to the state where individuality is but a momentary creation experienced in oneness. You can experience yourself as an aspect of God, an instrument in the symphony of life, and at the same time, you are experiencing God. When you have achieved this perspective, it is never lost, and connection to self is never quite the same again. In the words to "Amazing Grace":

I once was lost, and now am found,
was blind and now I see.

'Twas grace that taught my heart to fear,
and grace my fears relieved.
How precious did that grace appear,
the hour I first believed.

That initial connection to all consciousness is so precious, so meaningful and important, that we at once know that this is the answer to all our searching—this is "the way, the truth, and the life." We are only shadows of our true selves before we obtain this wisdom—this knowing.

From Matisse, speaking for the herd:
We, and I mean all of us, know truth at all times. It tends to get weighted down, lost in matter, so the more heavily rooted you are in the physical plane, the less you will recognize truth—not the physical-plane, mass-mind belief truth, but the *universal* truth. Humans have their own unique belief system, which only holds true for humans on the physical plane. You are all heavily

invested in the earth experience and profoundly limited by those beliefs. For us there is only life, not death—death is of the ego only (a very good thing, as far as we are concerned). There is only truth; lies are a human invention. There is only good. Evil, as well, is a human mind belief—it does not exist for the rest of creation. Everything is in constant transition. There are no days, months, years, hours, past, present, or future, and all is space. We are not in, on, over, or above—we just are . . . always. Isness, Beingness, Oneness, and ALLness are concepts we understand. The more you hold on to, own, contain, and attach to, the more work you make for yourself, and the more pain you experience when movement (which brings separation) occurs.

All life belongs to the ALL. You cannot hold your breath and live, and you cannot hold the breath of ALL, which is life, still, for a time. It is constantly breathing and exchanging. As all of our breath mingles with the breath of the earth, we are all united.

We are all *one* living, breathing, growing, and evolving organism.

Like Christ's wilderness experience, there is nothing that could be offered to us to replace that incredible lightness of being, that indescribable joy of communion with the ALL and through the ALL. It can only be found in reflection and contemplation, and is facilitated by the quiet and simplicity of the natural world. There it is, alive and well, and the natural way of being for all who would open to it.

LOST
by Kevin Ryan

Where are you going
Along
Alone
Winding among her
Sunshine beams
Holding on tight
To fears
Embrace
Hiding among her
Endless seams
Buried in electronic
Noisy chatter
Numb among her
Beautiful dreams.

Temptation and Sacrifice

From Prima, speaking for the herd:

Temptation and sacrifice can only be experienced from an ego state. When one is all there is, these devices do not exist. Animals certainly have no concept of these, and of course, humans put this down to lack of intelligence or a smaller brain. It is strange how humans dissect brains to determine the capacity of what they call *intelligence*, and yet it seems the true variant is in fact elusive and has no relation to the weight of the organ or the size of its individual parts. As my animals tell me, it is *mind*, not brain, that is the important factor, and connection to mind exists long after the brain has turned to dust.

Temptation and sacrifice are experienced by the "brain" discerning the collective human consciousness. Humans relate to a story that has long been alive in their culture, a story of sin and limitation, lack and greed. They believe that since we (the created ones) are all individual entities struggling to survive this ordeal called earth-life, that there are two choices: We are either tempted by evil or we sacrifice for good.

Since they are not really sure that this story is in fact true, they mostly give in to temptation and do the evil deed of taking for themselves at the expense of others. They sin, then they confess their sins, and are well on the road to sacrifice. Humans enjoy the intellectual stimulation of this game. I suppose it's like exercising their brain muscle to keep it fit.

There are no opposites when all is one. From that perspective it would be like taking from yourself to give to yourself—what would be the point? I would suggest that maybe because their brains are bigger, they need more exercise to keep them from getting flabby.

The whole organ idea is interesting as well. Consciousness is in all organs. It is not like the brain that thinks and directs all the organs; it is more like a democracy: Sometimes the liver is in charge, sometimes the heart, and the brain is directed to do its job accordingly. Consciousness is equally present in each facet of life—each cell, each organ, and each being. It is how we open to that consciousness that determines our experience.

When humans perceive themselves as finite beings subject to the laws of the physical plane, that is where their consciousness lives and grows. Humans, like one giant organ, determine the rules for their existence.

There is not enough for all of us. We must struggle, we will be tempted, and we must sacrifice—all bad news, very much like a game of chess. All is hidden and the biggest brain wins . . . Wow! We don't understand the energy you expend in solving a riddle that does not in fact exist.

Whew . . . this little excerpt from Prima demonstrates her mission: to illuminate mankind. She does sound somewhat disdainful. Interestingly, the more I am able to share the horses'

understanding, and the more easily I access Universal Truth, the more apologetic I feel for being human. From a higher perspective, we really do appear as mice in a maze. When someone moves our cheese, we all scurry, most of us mindlessly fighting to survive. If we could somehow teleport to a viewing station high above the maze, we would be able to see more clearly and determine the wisest path to take. It seems the more deeply we penetrate the human myth, the more mired and confused we become. Our lifestyles have become so unnatural. We live not only far from the earth and sky, but in toxic boxes, eating food laden with chemicals and irradiating ourselves with all our electric gadgetry. How could we possibly experience a clear thought? The only way out of the maze is to take a sabbatical and remove ourselves from the human jumble. Flying to a big hotel on a busy beach, dining at restaurants, and keeping in touch with cell phones and computers just won't do it. Sometimes I feel very depressed thinking that there really is no way out. There are far too many of us and we're far too greedy. Our drive for profit causes us to force animals and plants into our unhealthy, overcrowded conditions. They become toxic and the cycle continues.

> Our drive for profit causes us to force animals and plants into our unhealthy, overcrowded conditions. They become toxic and the cycle continues.

I believe the only way out is not from a physical but from a spiritual perspective. We have found ourselves in this mess because we have lost that spiritual perspective.

From Diva, speaking for the herd:

We animals have no desire to interfere with what we understand to be perfection, and we are wise enough to know that the only true and lasting form of influence is by example. We are creatures of peace. We are not dependent on you for our survival; rather, you are dependent on us. Do you think we would have a problem living on the earth if we were left to our own devices? You make us dependent when you confine us as you confine yourselves. Why do you live in unnaturally small places and allow other humans to take care of you? Because you can no longer take care of yourselves. life is all choice You have covered the earth with concrete, you dump poison on the land and in the water, and then you feed it to yourselves and your children. You feed it to the animals and then you eat them. How intelligent is that?

We are not dependent on you, Man; we choose to help you, and through you we can help the earth. How far off the path would you have wandered without animals to remind you of a simpler way? We teach by example. We offer truth and wisdom.

Look how we live in the wild. Do you see animals fighting to obtain more territory than is necessary for their survival do you see us lining up for welfare? Do we kill ourselves by overeating or ingesting chemicals? Do we work day and night so that we can have lots of paper in the bank and no time to enjoy it? We give up our freedom for a greater good. We are unconditional in the love and generosity of spirit that we extend to all life. We know our connection to each other and life itself, and we know that life cannot exist in isolation. It is symbiotic. If we lose a vital organ in the body, it dies, no matter how well the rest functions.

Wake up, Man, from this distorted dream that you are dreaming. You are alone in your illusion. Examine the analogy of man as a vital organ in the body of the earth—let us say the liver—which has numerous functions that are essential to the body. The liver has grown out of all proportion and is covered with a cancerous growth that is not only affecting the organ itself, but also the survival of the body dependent upon it. The individual cells of the liver, each with their own intelligence, are running in all directions; they have lost their connection to the unified whole. They are no longer in touch with the wisdom of the liver itself, and they are now at cross-purposes. The other organs go about their lives, functioning with their individual intelligence and in concert with the other organs, providing the systems that nourish and support the body as a whole. The liver, however, is no longer performing its necessary function for the health and vitality of the body. Should the other organs fight with the liver and compromise it even further, or should they try to maintain harmony in hopes that the liver will eventually regain its health?

The only way we can expand our vision and reconnect with the rest of the earth is to remove the human clutter and revisit our roots. We need to take time out in the country, close to nature and removed from our unhealthy lifestyle. We need to walk, to connect, to contemplate in the company of nature and animals. We need to let go of our judgment, our biases against all things not human. If we can be clear and open, truth will come to light.

Deep within us, the memory lingers of when we were still one with God and all life, not separate and alone.

From Limited Edition (L.E.), speaking for the herd:

The animals are content to go back to the Garden; it is only man who worships power, and power over material things is transitory. We have no need of it. Our possessions are few, but they are essential for immortality: Connection to God and all his creation; truth, which means a snake must not try to pretend he is anything other; and fidelity, to all that is good, to all that is God. Evil is a figment of man's imagination; when he veers from the path of what he knows to be good, he perceives a need for punishment, and he punishes himself. It is all his game, and as long as he enjoys the playing, what can we do to help? We are always ready for support, and that is why historically that has been our relationship. We have far more to offer, but as they say: "You can lead a horse to water but you can't make him drink." You can lead a man to pasture, but you can't make him eat.

In order to be a steward, you must be committed to caring for all life. *Caring* means respecting individual rights and freedoms, helping creatures grow to the fruition of individual truth. You cannot call yourself a steward when you bend the rules to accommodate your own personal gain. The world would be well and happy without human intervention.

Man, let us teach you what *stewardship* means. There are few of you who give it more than lip service. On one level you aspire to higher ideals, and on another you succumb to your greed. Let us remind you of a simpler way, one that is more rewarding by far, and one that is yours forever. The means are available, but it requires a huge commitment and sacrifice on your part. In order to have what is really worth having, you have to give it first.

It is all a balance, and the scale is not weighted in your favor at the moment.

When you spend time in the quiet, sincerely in search of truth, you will find it; you will remember it, for it is there in your soul. Instead of coming to us with agendas, come to commune—to just spend time in our presence. We are waiting for your invitation to interact as wise beings. We will not let you down. Climb on our backs and let us take you places that you have yet to discover. It is there in the unstructured time that true wisdom is found.

The only hope you have of changing the path you have chosen is to go back to the Garden and make a new decision. Instead of choosing the knowledge of good and evil, choose to be unaware of its existence. Go back to the place where you were one with all the creatures and God, and vow to never seek beyond the perfection of that moment.

You are confused and lost. All of your seeking has led nowhere, so let us help you find your way back.

The world you have crafted is in a state of disaster. People killing people over distorted belief systems; natural disasters wrought by misdirected consciousness. We animals are trying to hold the truth for the planet, but you humans are many and you hold powerful disbeliefs. You could just co-create your way out of this physical-plane experience! It seems like too little too late, but the only way it will change is one mind at a time. You must seek to remember—*re-member*. One mind influencing another, until a chain reaction occurs and all will be rejoined in truth. You are all—we are all—members of a world based on group belief. What we know the world to be will occur in matter. At present we are at cross-purposes—Man, and all the rest of the planet. Before it is too late, let us help you; let us help each other find our way back to the Garden.

Temptation and sacrifice are recurring themes in human life. We reach moments in our understanding when spiritual truth is somehow obvious, then our distorted mass belief seems to fade, and in the ensuing peace, we vow never to be tempted to the point where we forget this truth again. My animals tell me:

> To have your life you must give your life. True renunciation embodies absolute trust, absolute truth, and complete surrender. True clarity and connection are found in the quiet of the voice and of the mind. How can you hear when you chatter ceaselessly? How can you know the truth when you think your truth is all that matters?
>
> Cats, dogs, and horses have been your companions for millennia. We have surrendered our fate into your keeping—such is our trust in you. We know your hearts and your spirit, and we know that when you are in your hearts and your spirits, you are free. It is your minds that limit and confuse you. Turn off the chatter, let go of the confusion, and allow the stillness—the quiet—to fill you with its peace. The peace is within us all, but you revisit it only in moments. Stay a while longer. Let us take you there and sit beside you in communion and worship of this most precious gift. It is in this place where we are all connected in one consciousness and one truth, the place of Isness where we can speak with our hearts and share in the memory of our true kinship with each other and life itself. We are all children of the earth, seeded from the heavens where the ALL shines eternally. We are

eternally spiritually free, and when the memory awakens, we become fully actualized spiritual beings on this and all planes. We must give all to have all. That is the secret.

. . . And the sacrifice.

We are all on a journey toward our own personal epiphany. Some of us are on a mission, and others are in no hurry at all. We are told in the Bible: "In all thy ways acknowledge him, and he shall direct thy paths. . . . Ask and it shall be given unto you . . . seek and ye shall find . . . knock and the door shall be opened . . ."

The only way we can expand our vision and reconnect with the rest of the earth is to remove the human clutter and revisit our roots.

The simple truth is that once we have touched or been touched by God, our lives will never be the same. Our perspective as a separate being, an individual identity with a short life span on earth, is forever changed. Suddenly we see God in all life, feel God in all life, and know that the intimate connection offered by our intuition is in fact God's will for our life. The Christ within us is born, and it is no longer the little "i" but the big "I" that lives through us and as us. We become co-creators with God, and being so closely connected, we are no longer subject to the inventions of the ego. When one knows God in all life, it is not possible to want something for yourself that you would not want for all creation. We have been given absolute love, freedom, truth, wisdom, peace, and joy. Our joy is dependent upon experiencing the love of God shining through the eyes of all life.

Our life becomes a free flow of giving and receiving God and experiencing God; and God in turn finds pleasure in his

creation. Life is no longer a mental exercise—it is no longer a struggle to survive.

In the words of Thomas Merton:

It is in the ecstasy of pure love that we arrive at a true fulfillment of the First Commandment, loving God with our whole heart and our whole mind and all our strength. Therefore, it is something that all men who desire to please God ought to desire—not for a minute, nor for half an hour, but forever. It is in these souls that peace is established in the world.

They are the strength of the world, because they are the tabernacles of God in the world. They are the ones who keep the universe from being destroyed. They are the little ones. They do not know themselves. The whole earth depends on them. Nobody seems to realize it. These are the ones for whom it was all created in the first place. They shall inherit the land.

They are the only ones who will ever be able to enjoy life altogether. They have renounced the whole world and it has been given into their possession. They alone appreciate the world and the things that are in it. They are the only ones capable of understanding joy. Everybody else is too weak for joy. Joy would kill anybody but these meek. They are the clean of heart. They see God. He does all that they want, because He is the One Who desires all their desires. They are the only ones who have everything that they can desire. Their freedom is without limit. They reach out for us to comprehend our misery and drown it in the tremendous expansion of their own innocence that washes the world with its light.

Come, let us go into the body of that light. Let us live in the cleanliness of that song. Let us throw off the pieces of the world like clothing and enter naked into wisdom. For this is what all hearts pray for when they cry: "Thy will be done."

HER SMILE
by Kevin Ryan

Ten thousand
sun-glittering jeweled studs
on soft white forms
reflect in the iris
of life's perfect eye

a smile

as yours upon our pillow.

Baptism

It is a long, winding road to reach the point of being baptized in the name of Christ, meaning that God, manifest in His entire splendor on the physical plane, is now manifest in us. I was brought up in the United Church of Christ and baptized as a baby. Throughout my life I have always made the sign of the cross and baptized all I love in Christ's name. This, of course, includes all creatures, not just humans. Choosing to be baptized and accepting baptism is the crowning event in a personal journey—a commitment to God made when one fully understands that commitment.

I chose to be baptized again in my early forties. I had long been an initiate, not particularly in any one religion, but in the contemplation of God. Many years before, I had learned to meditate, I had experienced several intimate encounters with the ALL, read everything I could get my hands on in metaphysical books, and surmounted most of my fears; I was ready.

My husband Kevin and I were invited to experience a profoundly moving, four-day encounter-type experience called "Choices: Adventures of a Lifetime," which was designed to lead to a baptism service. I was ready and armed with huge expectations

and anticipation. The event was to be held at the Harrison Hot Springs Resort & Spa in British Columbia, a place I'd loved to visit with my parents as a young girl.

Kevin and I were given a list of do's and don'ts when we arrived. Being an enlightened being, I quickly tallied the reasoning behind such and decided that I would, contrary to the rules, share a room with my husband, and although I didn't smoke, I would still partake of my wine with dinner. When one of the leaders asked the group of over a hundred participants whether anyone had objections to their rules, I, of course, was the only one who raised my hand. I objected to the "no sex, no drinking" rule, as I believe that anything in moderation is not detrimental. As I was the only one objecting, the facilitator did not have a problem, and I glared at my husband for being so meek.

> Being baptized simply becomes a calling, an insatiable hunger and thirst for all things of God.

That was only the beginning. As the days unfolded, we were given various visualization exercises designed to try and dislodge any experience we'd had that could block us from being our true selves. My partner was a big, burly marshmallow of a man, just out of rehab, and he cried his way through several boxes of Kleenex while I loved him unconditionally and kept passing the tissues.

I objected to some of the exercises—one in particular where we were all figuratively dying had to figuratively save some people—but not others by giving them magic beans, of which we only had five. People were getting hysterical when others chose not to give them their beans (I told them that they didn't in fact need the beans—they were saved by the virtue of their belief—and I managed to quiet a few of the sobbing, unsaved souls).

I became a little militant when we were given nametags, which were all demeaning. One person was a non-achiever, one was a master-manipulator . . . you get the gist. Everybody had to be criticized and defend their position, and at that point we lost some of the more-sensitive participants. Because I wasn't able to say anything but constructive criticism, I was ostracized to my hotel room where, lo and behold, my nametag fell off when I bent over to take off my shoes. Coming from my belief system, this was God prompting me to follow my intuition. I quickly turned over my tag, on which was written MASTER-MANIPULATOR, and wrote a new label: GOD.

Oh, was I in trouble when I returned to the group. We were all participating in an exercise in which one person was the "pig in the middle." The "pig" was surrounded by several group members and "crucified" until they broke down or defended their position. Talk about taking on the Christ and speaking your truth. I was examined by all of my group sequentially; the higher-up members of the group, and then, the higher-ups of the higher-up, until I eventually got to Reverend Forrest Taylor, the recognized man of God who was, in fact, very closely connected to him in my opinion. After being questioned at length by Forrest, I was declared authentic and anointed. Wow . . . I had passed with flying colors, and it was the culmination of years of spiritual study.

By our request, Forrest baptized Kevin, my daughter, Francesca, and I in the Harrison Hot Springs pool. I absolutely knew in my heart that this was an honor bestowed by God. Baptism, I

believe, is a ceremony that recognizes our choice to wear the cloak of Christ in this mission we take on for God, this sojourn on the physical plane. The cloak of Christ not only allows us to rise above the confines of the physical plane, but also, by its merit, ordains us to testify for God.

Don't get me wrong—this does not make us perfect. In fact, we often plunge back into the human abyss. Being baptized simply becomes a calling, an insatiable hunger and thirst for all things of God. Nothing ever again can make us happy if it does not come via our God connection. This can be tortuous, as in the early stages when we can become inconsolable at what appears to be separation from God. Over time we learn that there is no real separation, just the appearance of it. Even the appearance of separation can be a formidable foe, however, raising its ugly head much too often, until finally, we are able to recognize it for what it is and can tell it to "get thee hence."

Knowing we are on our path, and anticipating an outcome that is grander and more perfect than our fondest dream, is to truly live life as the wonderful adventure that it is.

Fear is another stumbling block. Even though all of our human vices are still in existence, after baptism, we just know better. One by one we must "run naked" into each and every vice until the light has illuminated all of our darkness and clarified all of our confusion. This is a lengthy process and it took me decades to accomplish. This doesn't mean I am done, but at least I have put a good portion of it to rest, and an overwhelming measure of contentment is mostly present in my life. Certainly there is little need for competition or struggle, as I am filled with a knowing

and unconditional acceptance that every individual path is perfect and unique, and I am unfailingly guided along mine. I see God in all life and want only that perfection to unfold for all of creation. There is nothing more rewarding than observing and enjoying God's joy in all life.

When one is truly living life from the perspective of Isness, then our life purpose becomes God's purpose, and we are not only in alignment with God's will, but we are also aware of that will as a vital, evolving energy. Then, no matter how small or how simple the task, we are aware while doing it that this is God's will for us. There is an excitement, a moment of suspense that envelops all that we do, knowing ourselves to be part of a larger idea. We are aware of playing a significant role, as we are each important to God's plan, and at the same time, the outcome is somehow just beyond our grasp. Knowing we are on our path, and anticipating an outcome that is grander and more perfect than our fondest dream, is to truly live life as the wonderful adventure that it is.

> From Diva, speaking for the herd:
> There is wisdom in the path of least resistance, and that is the path we take. Originally, when we became partners with Man, it was a benefit to us both. We were respected, and we chose to stay in relationship with Man. We continue to make that choice, not so much for our own personal benefit, but for the benefit of the earth. You humans must learn balance; you must learn to walk the path of least resistance. You must temper your aggression so that it does not become counterproductive to your existence as a species, and to the existence of the web of life that you

are dependent on for your survival. You, Man, are not as intelligent as you believe. You have a saying about biting the hand that feeds you, and yet you bite your own hand.

When horses display aggression, it is for the purpose of maintaining the survival of their herd. There is an order and a reason to it. Man would do better to follow his intuition over his intelligence. He has forgotten his connection with spirit, with the wisdom that creates harmony and balance.

Consider the magnitude of the force of gravity, or the centrifugal force of the rotation of the earth on its axis, or its revolution around the sun. Consider conception and the force that causes matter to flow into myriad, intricate patterns, and those patterns that interact with each other and the earth itself in perfect precision. Man cannot come close to understanding that wisdom, yet he tries to influence his own small sphere; just look at the damage he does by exercising that influence.

Animals live in connection with God's will. They, unlike us, do not consider or choose an alternative. Our ultimate freedom and baptism in the name of Christ depends upon this submission to God's will as it manifests through our intuition.

When we are connected with God's will and have cemented that relationship over time, we reach a point where we can dwell in that place—a point where we need only periods of communion to maintain that connection. We find this communion in the sabbatical, the day of rest, where we dwell in our relationship with God. Then we can go out into the world and co-create with God while still maintaining that relationship. We can then be free to enjoy the excitement of participating in God's dream. We become free God Spirits who can travel beyond time and substance to places we previously had no access to when we were rooted on the physical plane. If you were to examine this relationship from an earth perspective, we are free to travel with our thoughts into the future, the past, to the world of spirit, where existence transcends our ideas of time. We become fully actualized microcosms of The ALL, knowing and fulfilling his will in all things.

Chapter 6

Lesson in Aloneness

Almost seven years ago, when my husband and I left our busy lives, large family, and hosts of friends to relocate to our secluded ranch, it was like plunging from the highest diving board into a still, clear pool. *Splash!* For a while, I felt like I was underwater, swimming around in a glass fishbowl while the rest of the world was somehow functioning on the other side of the glass. Kevin was commuting to the old world where he maintained a foothold on shore. I was alone in the wilderness with only my animals for company. It was a beautiful, pristine paradise, like walking in the Garden of Eden—the natural world untouched by man sparkled with energy. My animals were my constant companions: seven horses (at the time), three dogs, and a cat, and the silence and songs of a world devoid of humans became my comfort and my solace. There were, of course, moments of intense aloneness. I was separated from my own kind, thrust into a world where none of the human laws applied. There were no niceties, no subtleties, no pretense—just unvarnished absolute truth, and quiet. Being human and accustomed to noise, I began to talk to myself

and to the animals—for company, I suppose. Nevertheless, I experienced many episodes of acute loneliness.

> From my journal:
> Elizabeth, where are you now? Why do you think I've left you? Your aloneness is a gift. It's important. You must be alone to truly know me. No phone, no way out, no one to lean on. Go into the pain; don't look for anyone but me to help you out. This is forced seclusion and it will be worthwhile. Everyone must go through the fire to refine his or her spirit. You are alone; you are born alone, and you die alone, but you have me; you are me. As with all things, stop struggling against it. Your aloneness is time to be with me. When you stop struggling against it, you won't feel alone. You of little faith; one day you are here, and the next, you're floundering again. Jump in, feel the pain; it is purification. Don't look to others to help. They are mirrors reflecting back what you need to learn, and it is you who must learn it. They cannot save you from your lessons. Remember: To have all, you have to give all . . . and I mean all. I must come first. But, my dear, you are almost there. Christ went into the wilderness for forty days and fasted just before he was tested, and it was all given to him. You are doing fine; you are loved by the most important person to be loved by. Again, I tell you to trust and allow. You are O.K. (Of the Kingdom). *Go within*.

It appeared I was struggling through some kind of initiation. Solitude was to be my salvation. Days became weeks, weeks became months. God was my only companion, and yet, as much as I was given insight through a dialogue that was ever available in my mind, I began to experience a God that was at once beyond words and thoughts, a presence that spoke through the heartbeat, the breath of all life. It seemed that the more I was content to rest in the silence and abandon the need to define experience in human words and concepts, the more I began to absorb a broader definition that in fact defied definition at all. The very word *God* implies a sole identity, somewhat human, seemingly male. The God I began to identify with was a God who defied description—a wholeness, a oneness, an ALLness—or as I finally understood, the God that was inherent to all life, the ALL.

> I gained a whole new perspective on solitude. It became clear that when life is viewed from the higher, more expansive viewpoint of the ALL, this moment in time loses its importance.

When one speaks of the ALL, there can be no division, no hierarchy—just sameness, oneness, ALLness, and Isness.

This is the God who spoke to me in my aloneness, who spoke with a voice that was all sound and yet no sound at all. I was simply implanted with a vision, and I absorbed the contents. I had only to touch the ocean, as the horses spoke of earlier, and I became the sea. It was within and without, and I was integral to its composition—a molecule of water that was water itself.

Once assimilated, it became obvious that having let go of the human perspective, the brightness of the ALL shone, unfettered by a finite comprehension. It simply was, and I, and all life, was finite, in the sense of individual, yet infinite in the greater sense, in the expression of ongoing ALLness forever. Man speaks of the word of God where animals simply experience God.

My horse Epona explains these horse beliefs:

You, Man, have written a Bible—a code of ethics for humanity. That code of ethics has been translated into the most unethical document of all time. It was said to be the word of God, but God is not divided against himself. God *is*. That does not imply a need to define, or manipulate, or act in any way that is incongruous with God's nature of Isness.

Do we act in any way other than the God made manifest in our being? We have no desire but to reflect the glory of God's beingness in the individual beauty and majesty of our spirit. You will not see a horse trying to change or redirect the flow of spirit. We succumb to all we encounter. We are prey animals, and it is an interesting play on words, that we in fact *pray*, which means we ask for guidance from our source, and follow without question the guidance we are given. Man is forever questioning. Predators are animals that live on prey animals. Not only do you depend on us to maintain your physical life, but you also depend on us for the life of your spirit.

We sustain ourselves with the energy of the earth and the heavens. There is an equal flow of energy that offers balance in our lives. Without the interface that we afford, without the balance that we offer, man would be forever lost between the two worlds. We offer ourselves in body and in spirit, in hopes that you might know the wisdom of that true communion. When humans worship, they eat the flesh and drink the blood of Christ; it is a ceremony to confirm their commitment to the possibility of life through Christhood, the full possibility of God made manifest on the physical plane.

That is the value of our belief. We believe in the possibility of God's perfection in all creation, and we live our belief. We do not try to change that possibility in any way; we are true to our guidance and God's will on earth as it is in heaven. So be it. A men.

I gained a whole new perspective on solitude. It became clear that when life is viewed from the higher, more expansive viewpoint of the ALL, this moment in time loses its importance. When viewed from life's summation, how can the minuscule aspects of an individual life merit more than a contribution to the whole?

An example: Fred Smith was born, earned a degree in physics, raised a family, amassed some assets, died, and left them to his family. Who cares in the grand scheme of things? When Fred returns to the ALL and accounts for himself, has this spark of light made the ALL shine brighter? Or has it simply burnt its supply of energy and extinguished itself, needing to go back to its source for more supply? There are few brilliant sparks that shine through the muck and mire of the material plane, but those who truly do are a clear facet on the brilliant diamond of the ALL, touching the world with their light and offering nourishment and growth that in turn feeds the ALL, making it grow brighter. The crystal clarity in this plan is that the ALL is nothing without us. To express on the physical plane, the ALLness must explode into matter in a burst of creative genius, each individual fragment containing the

> This is the God who spoke to me in my aloneness, who spoke with a voice that was all sound and yet no sound at all. I was simply implanted with a vision, and I absorbed the contents.

complete compliment of its creator, even as it exists as a single cell. Important to all life, that cell must tap into the energy of the ALL to exist and to exchange. Inflow and outflow must be balanced in order for life to continue.

We must go and rest in the silence and truly contemplate life's mysteries for the answers to appear. If we are constantly surrounded by the chatter of society, inundated with mass mind, we become lost—generic in our thought processes and never discovering our individual and unique selves. Aloneness is not only important for the development of our individuality; it also takes us beyond the identification with our species to the much larger community with all life. We must lose ourselves to find our greater selves.

To expire is to die; to inspire is to live. Inspiration is to breathe in the genius of the ALL—we incorporate it and then translate that inspiration into a unique interpretation through our individuality. All life is dependent on this connection with our source, and the more open and clear the connection, the more inspired we are. Creative force flows through us to the world, and then back from the world to become a larger and more embellished ALL. We are intimately connected. It is as if the ALL breathes out upon the world, a breath that is exchanged through all creation, then breathed in again by the ALL.

Lost in a mundane existence within a crowded city, we lose our awareness of the breath of life. How can we breathe deeply of polluted city air? How can we clear our heads of the constant hum of micro radiation and hear anything but the din of bustling industry? More and more humans are sensing the loss of their

natural connection to the earth, and desolate and confused, they are numbing themselves from the pain with more stimulation instead of retreat. The majority believes there is no salvation—we are doomed by the irony of our own desire.

The secret of our salvation is our intent. When we have hit the bottom, there is no way out other than to throw ourselves on the mercy of God. We must desire to know the truth of our existence more than we desire anything else. This is pure intent, and when our intent has been mobilized, there is no force more powerful. It is as if all of existence sits up and takes notice that we have finally asked the right question. it has been waiting forever for that question to be asked, and our heart's desire is the illumination found in the answer.

In a conversation with my brother the other day, we were discussing the dilemma of how a city person could achieve a connection with the natural world. Certainly most of us live with animals who are a clear conduit to their source. It is the unstructured time with them that brings results. We must be clear and open to their energy. They are the teachers and we are their pupils. Rather than throwing a ball or stick, to just sit in their company with our senses open and receptive, uncluttered by random thoughts, will over time bring a meditative clarity to our lives.

Yards and parks are other avenues, not always available to city people. We do have one unfailing resource available at all times, in all places: the sky, the very air itself, connected throughout the world and to all life. We are all dependent upon that one vital element for our connection to life. Contemplating the sky is a recreation and retreat that can take us instantly to meditative release and clarity. It is an immediate stress reducer connecting us with our source and sustenance. You only have to take a few moments to gaze at the sky and your consciousness will be expanded above and beyond the ordinary, the mundane, to a plane where dreams and visions are commonplace and all of your earthly problems are far below. No wonder the heavens have always been thought to exist in the sky.

An important milestone in our spiritual journey is accomplished in silence and solitude. We must question the reason for our existence, and then we only have to rest in the possibility of the answer. That rest is facilitated by moments of true connection and moment-by-moment wisdom; only then can clarity be gained. The result of our dedication to truth will eventually crystallize to form our unique identity, our individual elements, much like a snowflake or the facets of a diamond create a brilliance and beauty unlike any other.

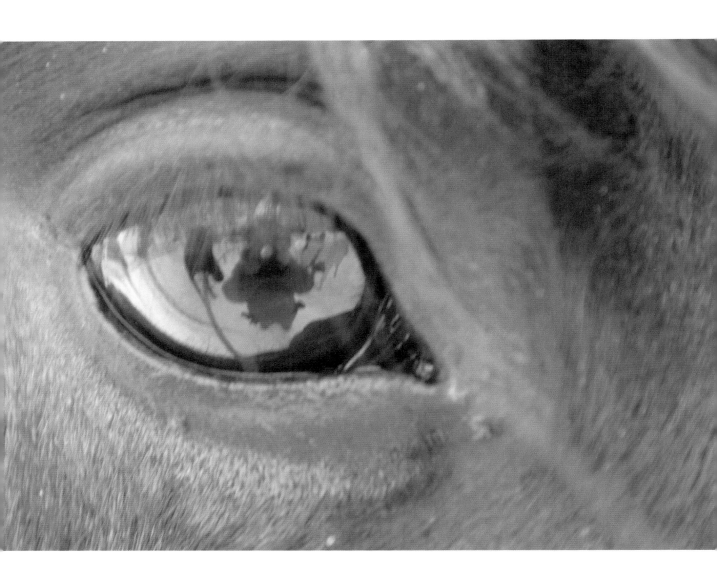

True Identity

We are prisms, all of us—all life focusing light through our bodies to become rainbows. It's interesting that humans tell the story of a pot of gold at the end of the rainbow. We are heir to infinite riches, wealth we need only imagine to receive. We have long ago forgotten our true Identity. We are all "I." Each individual life form speaks the word "I" and co-creates with God. *I am* is the resounding chorus in all life. How then can we express our individuality while still reflecting the whole?

The secret to discovering our true identity is found in the power of intention.

The physical plane is a hard, cruel teacher when we identify with our small selves. Our little egos are easily bashed and broken. Humans are amazingly resistant, however, and one can witness the full spectrum of disease, disadvantage, and suffering while still dragging ourselves through the mire of mass misbelief. It is heart-wrenching when we consider the torture some humans endure. When we are told that this experience is all self-imposed, we protest, asking how can this be true of the baby born crippled, or the child with cancer. God is cruel and uncaring . . . it is all his fault. Wrong! We have created this nightmare through human mass belief. Our thoughts make collective laws. The rules for being human have been agreed upon through the ages. We all believe in the parameters for our physical-plane existence. We believe this is a world of opposites: There is good and evil, joy and suffering. It's interesting that the rest of existence, the animals and plants, do not experience opposites. Most humans agree that the world is a mess; there is nothing we can do.

> From Premiere Edition, speaking for the herd:
>
> In one instant you can change the world. If man were to change his mind, one mind at a time, a chain reaction (like nuclear fission) would occur. Human minds like ours are all joined—it is the belief in isolation that creates the limits. Simply let these barriers go, and a far greater world will be yours, ours, in the communion of spirit as it has always been.
>
> That is the simple truth: You can affect your life with your thoughts, but beyond that narrow perspective you hold, nothing changes. The truth remains the same. There are two ends to the spectrum. Fear is at one end and it is false; love is at the other and it is all that is true.

The truth is, we are all God. It is only humans who have separated themselves from this knowledge. Why did humans want to separate? you may ask. Why not the animals?

From Premiere Edition (Prima), speaking for the herd:

Perspective is the key here. From your perspective, you think that you are the different ones, the superior species—the most like God. That is the story as you have told it—it is your story. We all have a story that is told from our own perspective. The difference is that animals are in agreement because they have not left the Garden (the place where all walk and talk with God). Humans believe in a human myth. It is the story that supports separation. Animals have a knowledge of good, or God. People wanted to create a perspective that would give them superiority . . . or so they thought. "Let us have evil, which is the opposite of what all other life understands." And they have boxed themselves into a corner. They have created another category, and, being the designers of their world, have made themselves a hell on earth.

The point is, we all view the world from our own perspective, with "our" being either singular or plural. Human/Humans. Horse/Horses. The difference is, humans believe in opposites; we believe in "sames." Every being sees the world through their own eyes; every species, through the eyes of their species. Animals interconnect species to species, to Man, and that is how we can help you. We can share our vision; we can show you paradise again.

You are the only species that has lost this connection, and therefore wrongly believe that you are separate and therefore superior. Just like in a flying change, when we horses change our lead midair, the lead is the perspective. Change your lead in midair and change your direction. It is that simple: As you believe, so will you experience life.

Spiritual masters stress the importance of not identifying with our little selves—our egos. When we view the world from this perspective, we are separate and alone. One cell in the body of humanity, a tiny part of a tiny being in the vastness of space. What is it that makes us special? It is not our physical being, one tiny cell afloat in the space of existence, buffeted by winds and currents, squashed by an accident of nature. The qualities that lend us greatness are found in our spiritual immortal selves, that part of us that will always be "I."

When we discover our true identity, our oneness through the creative life force that is immortal,

> We have long ago forgotten our true Identity. We are all "I." Each individual life form speaks the word "I" and co-creates with God.

omniscient, omnipresent, and unlimited, we awaken, or become enlightened. Our burdens are lifted; we no longer identify with mortality and limitation.

This is something I see animals accomplish in a very fluid way. They can be present in body, yet they are also able to leave that identity and expand to encompass their larger selves. We see this in animal instinct, the powerful force that protects each individual animal, its species as a whole, and all animals in general. You will not find an animal that ignores its instincts. Although humans are given intuition, the human version of animal instinct, we often ignore it. Usually this has harsh consequences and results in having to learn more lessons in the adventure playground of life.

We are amazingly resilient, but time and circumstance continue to beat away at us. While the strong keep struggling, the weak often fall by the wayside. That is until we, by chance or grace,

begin to discover that we can do nothing about our own selves; our salvation is found in our true identity. We sense that through our struggles there has been a guiding force that somehow nudges us in the direction of our highest good. This force has been our strength in adversity, our rudder in the storm. It has always been there, closer than our hands and feet. Yet somehow it is not until we have exhausted all of our other resources that we, broken and bleeding, beg for assistance. We speak the word and invite the power, and by our invitation and the power of the spoken word, the heavens open and we are saved.

> You will not find an animal that ignores its instincts. Although humans are given intuition, the human version of animal instinct, we often ignore it.

This experience always comes as a revelation; the long-forgotten memory of our true selves, our infinite power, surges like a tidal wave, engulfing our world, washing away all that exists in our limited human beliefs and revealing that there is no limitation. There are no opposites. There is only one truth, one life, and that is God's within all creation. You, being filled with that God-force, are heir to all God's facets. You are immortal. You must only speak the word and the world, which belongs to you, will change. You are both the experiencer and the experience itself!

Strangely enough, this experience—meaning our identification with and memory of our true selves—usually comes and goes like a flash of lightning. We are not able to contain this high level of vibration; the lightness must rise to the light, and we are left changed forever, yet somehow still trapped in our heaviness.

We create in matter, both in our human mass-mind consciousness and in our spiritual true identity. We begin to confuse the

two and create the next round of miscommunication and mistakes. At this point the knowledge we have gained will not allow us to hide from the fact that we are the creators of our world. Yet we are confused. One day we remember the secrets of the universe, and the next we are tossed like a fish to the shore to flounder in the wet sand.

The animals tell me that Man, being egocentric and left-brained, creates in matter by invention rather than intention.

From Nune, my cat:

We animals create with intention and focus, not invention, when it comes to affecting matter, by the Law of Attraction, when we focus on an outcome it manifests in matter without harming or changing substance in any way. You humans create new substances that are outside the natural order, and play havoc with the earth. You have relied on your brains to the point where you have lost your connection to Universal Mind. People, with their desire to understand or to know how everything works, dissect the world around them and impose laws by consensus that govern the physical plane. The secret of these laws lies in the consensus, or group belief. They have simply given themselves limitations that would not otherwise have existed. This world is just as we believe—each animal, vegetable, and mineral holds the world order in their belief system. We animals are working hard to hold the planet together with a clarity and purity of thought made possible by our connection to the spiritual plane. We offer this understanding to humans, who catch glimpses of truth when their minds are quiet enough to receive it.

Again, the secret is to stay connected to the guiding presence of our spiritual or higher selves. Just as instinct is the presence of the creative life force in animals, so our intuition is that presence in mankind. We have only to repeatedly reach for that spiritual lifeline in order to maintain a presence that will vaporize the heaviness of our earthly experience. Much like turning on a light in a dark room, the truth of who we are illuminates the dark corners of our early journey, revealing that there is no darkness in the presence of light.

The world we understand and agree upon as humans is an illusion. Like Alice's adventure through the looking glass, we see darkness and distortion through the heaviness of our physical plane.

Why did we choose this experience? Because we love God; because we are love expressing in matter; and because we, being the seed of God planted in the earth, will grow to become the flowers of God, individual, breathtakingly beautiful and unique in every way. We will struggle through the soil, fed and watered by the miracle of life, and eventually reach the light to express our brilliance and radiance, which is the glory of our creator.

Thomas Merton, from *New Seeds of Contemplation*:

No two created beings are exactly alike. And their individuality is no imperfection. On the contrary, the perfection of each created thing is not merely in its conformity to an abstract type but in its own individual identity with itself. This particular tree will give glory to God by spreading out its roots in the earth and raising its branches into the air and the light in a way that no other tree before or after it ever did or will do.

REMEMBER
by Liz Mitten Ryan

There is a story to be told
One that has been floating on the breeze
One that whispers softly to all that will listen
It caresses us gently and cradles us in its arms.
It is the story of our provenance
Our home and our hearts' desires.
We can hear it if we spend some time in silence
Among the animals and the trees
Alone with the earth and sky.
It is there we will hear it in the voice that speaks without words
The voice that echoes in all hearts . . .
Remember.

Chapter 8

"Isness"

Today, in this moment, I am the miraculous child of God; I am the ALL and the everything. I have no limits. I am love, joy, freedom, truth, wisdom, and abundance in expression. I remember! These moments of reconnection are exhilarating and life-changing. Some people have never experienced them, others once or twice, and some, like a moth to a flame, spend their life circling endlessly around the light. Will we ever experience more than a moment's comfort from the perspective of our earthly confines?

I think that the rules for being human are so deeply engrained that our body walls have become our fortress, nearly impervious to all that would challenge their integrity. Our perceived identity is dependent on the protection of our ego at all costs. This separationist belief is the cause of all our struggles; we struggle against life, each other, and ourselves. All that threaten our understanding are deemed to be dangerous and must be fought. If we should succumb to an onslaught, our sense of self would be destroyed, and with it, the very life of our ego being only a sense of self.

What if the worst actually happened? What if our sense of self was challenged and we were able to see the sense of the other side?

Almost everything is the other side to the ego. We are simply one point in the universe of existence, and all that is beyond that point is beyond us. How limiting that belief system seems when we imagine ourselves outside of and beyond that dot we call "us."

The interesting thing is that we have the power of imagination; we can dream, and oftentimes our dreams come true, when circumstances are right or focus is steady. Then, we are able to see beyond the illusion of this physical-plane existence.

Everyone has heard of the Law of Attraction: what we focus on, we attract. We have proven scientifically that we create in matter with our thought. So there are no hard-and-fast walls around material objects. All is fluid, flowing as we channel it with our thoughts. Why, then, would we hold to our belief in walls?

In *The Truth According to Horses*, my horse Prima directs her thoughts to people who believe beings are separate:

> We are all one—human, plant, animal, and rock. Every single little quark is united in the same cosmic soup. There are spaces but no boundaries. Boundaries are only thoughts.
>
> Humans think they must fight to survive: If you were to let go of your concerns for self even for a moment, the boundaries, being mere thoughts, would simply disappear. Then you would experience life as we do.

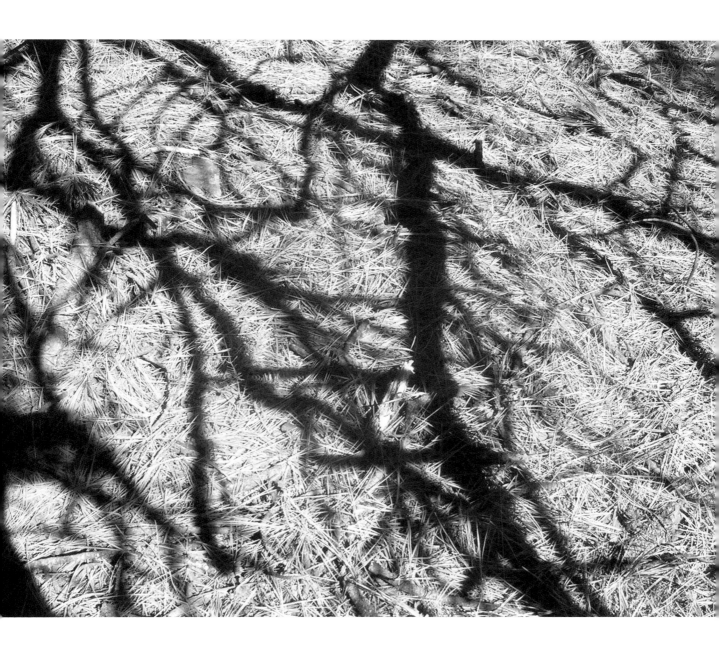

Animals, although they experience a clear sense of self, are not limited by it. They, by the nature of their instinct, are more strongly connected to that creative life force within their individual life in matter.

Having now spent ten years in their community, I have somehow been absorbed into their understanding. I say this from a third-person perspective, as I seem to have been encompassed by their beliefs and now exist in a place that is subject not only to horse mass-mind belief or consciousness, but also one that expands to include the mass-mind belief of all living creatures—meaning, I'm privy to the belief systems of animals and humans as individuals groups, and also the structural integrity of universal mind.

> I am the ALL and the everything. I have no limits. I am love, joy, freedom, truth, wisdom, and abundance in expression.

This state of experience is an extension of the brief moments we spend in the enlightened state, and is completely natural for animals and all who live in the Garden apart from human confines. Why have we convinced ourselves that we should have limits in a limitless universe? All other creatures sing and dance in unison; far above and beyond their individual identities, they encompass all of creation and vibrate with the pulse of life itself.

In our original state, before our fall from grace, mankind walked and talked with our creator and all creation. We were not separate and alone, but one with the Garden experience. We had the time then to reflect upon and absorb our surroundings. Have you ever sat upon a hill and experienced a sunset so glorious that you forgot your sense of self and became one with the earth and the sky . . . one with the entire perfection of that sunset? That is the way life

was for us so long ago, when we had no ambition to be, do, or have anything that was not already ours. We were connected in our thoughts to each other, and to all thoughts. There was only one thought throughout the earth—until, of course, we decided to separate and become an individual species, set apart and limited to that one identity. Why then would we choose to identify with one point, one little dot in the masterpiece of all creation?

Maybe because we believed this would make us different and unique; we could have something that was ours alone, separate and apart from all else.

> In our original state, before our fall from grace, mankind walked and talked with our creator and all creation.

Everything beyond our little dot would be outside or inside, to the left or right, north or south, warm or cold, compared to . . . oh my God, we have created polarity and opposites! This is great fun. We could even pretend to be other than what we were. Who would know, since all else was outside of us and no longer connected to our thoughts?

And so it began:

In the beginning was the word, and the word was with God, and the word was God. And the word was made flesh and dwelt among us and we beheld his glory.
—John 1:14

That was the true light, which lighteth every man that cometh into the world.
—John 1:9

*But as many as received him, to them he gave the power to become
the sons of God, even to them that believe in his name.*
                    —John 1:12

In *The Truth According to Horses*, the animals have another
version:

> *In the beginning was the word, and the word became bad.*
> *Bad because it spoke a lie. That lie was the light of men,*
> *And they believed it would give them power—*
> *A power over all creatures great and small;*
> *A power over each other.*
> *They were wrong.*
> *This huge mistake has cost them dearly.*
> *Generation after generation has inherited that original sin.*
> *The sin is greed.*
> *In our world, there is no such thing.*
> *Animals are truly in the moment,*
> *Something aspired to by seekers of truth.*
> *We have always been here to carry you, to ease your burdens.*
> *This is not only meant in the physical sense.*
> *Spend some time with us—we will show you what we mean.*

We have been enjoying this marvelous play we have created,
changing character and costume, but not with impunity. There
is a cost to our decision. The walls of individuality have become
so thick that we now find it difficult to escape. Another person,
or the world outside ourselves, can now cause us pain. Pain is the
opposite of pleasure and another facet of our creation. Now by
the nature of our encapsulated existence, we cannot escape the

pain. It thwarts us whenever we encounter something contrary to our personal pleasure. It consumes and becomes us.

Oh my God, what have we done? Our dream has now become a nightmare, and being the creative genius of our own production, we must think of a plan to escape. For a long time we have wandered down the hallways of the great theater, wearing the masks of both comedy and tragedy, entertaining ourselves and others who enjoy the world of pretense. Suddenly we realize that we have created a monster—a dragon that must be slain.

We have been enjoying this marvelous play we have created, changing character and costume, but not with impunity. There is a cost to our decision.

In the beginning of this book, *Isness* was defined as a knowing and a becoming, a fluent state of wisdom and grace that embodies all creation. If there is only one life force in all creation, then just maybe we, being the seed of that life force, are becoming that Isness no matter how hard we struggle. In nature, when a seed is planted, it can lie dormant until the right circumstance is mobilized, but with sunlight and water and good soil, it will eventually grow to become the flower and then the fruit that is inherent in its genetic structure.

It is interesting that we struggle against a force as wonderful and powerful as the force of love, knowing that it is the force that holds the universe together. Every day it moves the sun across the sky, fills the oceans and the rivers, and provides food and shelter for every living thing. Why is it we don't trust it? It is the very force of gravity that holds us to the earth; that holds our earth revolving around the sun; and the sun itself that is the energy required for all life. How can we be so dense as to understand the miraculous and yet forget it immediately? It must be the two sides of our brain, and having spent so much time in the left, the synapses have ossified.

How can we reach a state of Isness? Simply encourage the right side by spending more time there. How do we do this? By letting go of our concerns for achievement and personal glory, and by bathing in the glory of nature. There is nothing we can achieve in our earthly struggle that is incorruptible and eternal except all those attributes that are non-material and ethereal—ether-real. There is matter and ether, and the ether is the only substance that is real.

As *A Course in Miracles* (http://www.acim.org) suggests:

Nothing real can be threatened.
Nothing unreal exists.
Herein lies the peace of God.

Know this to be the foundation of our universe and rest lovingly in the miraculous power of Isness.

ROSE
by Kevin Ryan

In the morning sun
warm
gentle
A soft beauty
intense
enticing
Reaches into the soul
and calls.

Its scent
mists perception
With a sweetness
of untold depths
Vibrating
gently
A flower
in myriad shades of pink
and brilliant yellow
Fragile
On its verdant stem
of soft
thorns
The wild rose

L. I. F. E. Forever

Imagine you are only your thoughts. You have not yet chosen your character, or setting, or the other players in the marvelous production we call life, or L.I.F.E. (Love In Finite Expression). You are only your thoughts floating in a sea of pure possibility; you are the force of love itself, the most powerful creative force in the universe. You can be, do, have, and create anything you can imagine. What will you imagine?

This is the truth of our spiritual selves: We are ether; we are all that exists beyond the material plane, and our thoughts are the magnetic force that holds the universe together. As we think, we create. Much like the way a magnet drawn through iron shavings collects and shapes the iron in its path, our thoughts influence the tiniest building blocks of matter. Scientists observing quarks at the quantum level of physics are able to influence their movement and therefore obtain different results for the same experiment. It has been found that quarks don't in fact exist until we focus on them.

Matter is dense and heavy, and our influence at the quantum level takes time to manifest within the laws of matter, and is again influenced by the collective thoughts of human mass consciousness. That is what is holding us back. The human belief system is so weighted in matter from years of limited thinking. What we believe in, we see, and what we are afraid of, we choose not to see. Limited concepts such as evil, pain, and death hold our world captive. We have created the stage upon which we all are allowed to play.

What is interesting is that we all experience different results depending upon our individual belief systems within the greater consciousness of humanness. The other remarkable concept is that as our individual consciousness changes, the consciousness of humanity is changed as well.

On a larger scale there is the collective understanding of each species, each created thing within the larger playing field of the earth plane.

Horse mass consciousness has created a different world than has dog or whale consciousness, for example. All species, however, except for humans, agree on the general laws of consciousness. The only hope as I see it for humans to escape from the confines of their limited belief system is to spend unstructured time observing and absorbing the consciousness of animals and the natural world.

When I first began to spend time away from human influence in the company of my dogs, cats, and horses, it was an exercise in self-discipline to live without the soothing, affirming effects of the human perspective in pictures, print, and audio. Living in a wall tent with only my dogs and cats for company, I found myself without radio, television, newspapers, and phone. At the

beginning, the silence was difficult, and I spoke aloud to myself and the animals. I would follow my horse herd during the day, and gradually found myself enjoying the natural sounds of birds and insects and the contented snorts and nickering of my herd. I began to understand their language and became aware of the subtle inflection of different body parts, their focus and communication through facial expressions and pointed looks. I began to speak to them in their own language, as well as additional human words, which the herd began to understand. Over time our shared conversations became more complex. We were developing a language unique to horse/human hybrids, which we were becoming. I was accepted as one of the herd, with a special place as human-lead-mare (as opposed to horse-lead-mare, which already existed in the herd).

> The only hope as I see it for humans to escape from the confines of their limited belief system is to spend unstructured time observing and absorbing the consciousness of animals and the natural world.

There were different rules for the human-lead-mare, while at the same time I was applying new rules as to how I regarded horses. They were no longer strangers to me. I no longer would cringe at a lifted hoof or worry over being run down or attacked. We had become a family with shared values and customs. I loved them completely, and they loved me.

I find it interesting that people have preconceived ideas of how different animals should be treated, and most dictate that animals are less important than humans in every way. Why should humans get the roast beef and the dogs the leftovers? Why should animals the size of horses live in tiny cubicles, while humans live in 4,000-square-foot homes? The more I live with and connect to animals, the stranger I find these ideas. At the moment I have a baby bull living on my front porch by choice and taking over the doghouse and dog beds at every chance. I'm not sure he even knows he's a bovine, as when he's not playing dog, he's in the pasture with the ponies. My dogs all sleep on the couches, cats are welcome on the table, and all have specially prepared dinners and complete respect and love. I believe love is the product of familiarity. We grow to love those we choose to share our lives with: our family.

I have always been able to identify with other life forms and feel empathy and understanding for them. We are all spiritual equals who share the one creative force in all life—the force of love.

Because of the nature of the physical plane, each species must eat or be eaten, run or be eaten, take or have it taken from you. It is very convincing, this total immersion in matter. Yet always above and beyond the physical, we are aware of that place where our thoughts exist apart from all else. There, we are joined with all creation. There is only one thinker, one consciousness, and on the spiritual plane where we are no longer limited by the confines of a body, we can become instantly what we think about. There are only brief moments on the physical plane where we can forget ourselves and truly join with another being or experience. It is in those moments when we know Love In Finite Expression and can empathize with all of *life*. It is our beginning . . . our journey home . . . and our family forever.

UNSURE
By Kevin Ryan

What would be your greatest wish, I wonder.
Would it be for another, or others, or for yourself?
Material or spiritual,
An event or a state of being?

And what does one give to celebrate your being?
Where do I start?
Maybe a trinket
Or an accessory
Perhaps an event, although I tried that one.

A simple expression of how much you move me.
A testament of your beauty,
A witness to the music of your smile.

An act of giving something that moves your heart,
That opens it and brings joy.

What could that be?
It cannot be anything material
Too shallow for the heart.

What could that be?

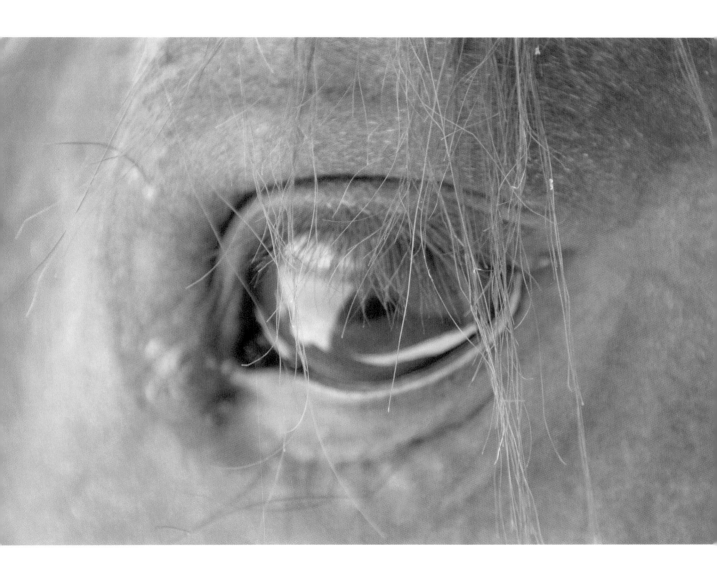

Sabbatical

A sabbatical is a rest from work. When God created the earth, he worked for six days and rested on the seventh. True connection is found when we are at rest. Our busy minds are not aspiring to achieve anything; we are open and we are quiet. This is the meditative state in which we connect with the ALL. As creative beings, our left brains are busy analyzing, processing, and directing our experiences. We desire to achieve all manner of things that will satisfy those desires. We can then be comfortable and at rest. The problem is that when we are operating from our left brains, there is little connection to the right side where Isness resides. Our true happiness is only possible when we are existing in that state of Isness, oneness, and wholeness—our true state of being. It is easy to get lost in the maze of physicality. The human mass consciousness has invented a Satan who is evil and tempts us with promising gifts that are transitory and cost us our soul. When we examine the parables of the Bible, there is always the evidence of temptation and salvation. Why is it we tell ourselves the same stories over and over in myths and fables? Even though we forget the morals, we somehow enjoy hearing them time and again.

The human experience has been called a deep sleep, a forgetting. It is truly a struggle between the forces of good and evil. As powerful creators, when we struggle against something, we give it power; our focus brings it into existence. It seems at this time that we humans are focused on the big, bad news—the sensational headlines are what captivate us. Our egocentric selves, with which we have identified for millennia, enjoy the fight for survival. They understand only their separateness, which in egocentric thought is their entire existence; namely, "me against the world"—lack and limitation as opposed to abundance and freedom. It tweaks the left brain where the cognitive functions enjoy the challenge.

It makes me wonder why I chose to be human since I have no interest in most left-brain activity. My energy resonates with the spiritual realms. I find that even in nature there are elements of physical-plane laws. We can witness pain and suffering from the human vantage point, and from our perspective of being invested in our egos, we experience the world with human emotion. I have both witnessed and been told by my animals that because they don't identify with an egocentric body, they are free to leave an experience which is threatening their physical being. It is again all in the perspective of whether you identify with or are just experiencing a creative expression.

Our busy minds are not aspiring to achieve anything; we are open and we are quiet. This is the meditative state in which we connect with the ALL.

When we are busy working out a plan, or when we are studying or learning or desiring any outcome that requires becoming something other than what we are, it demands a huge amount of effort. Why would we choose to expend that effort when all

is given to us? All is ours by the very nature of our oneness with God. It must stem from our suspicious nature, which is convinced that everything outside of us is a threat.

Kahlil Gibran in *The Prophet* states that:
Work is love made visible . . .
And what is it to work with love?
It is to weave the cloth with threads drawn from your heart, even as if your beloved were to wear that cloth.
It is to build a house with affection, even as if your beloved were to dwell in that house.
It is to sow seeds with tenderness and reap the harvest with joy, even as if your beloved were to eat the fruit.
It is to charge all things you fashion with a breath of your own spirit, and to know that all the blessed dead are standing about you and watching.

From that understanding, it can be seen that if our work is truly love made visible, then that in itself is a joy and a rest for our spirit. If every day we allow ourselves to be carried away in the flow, magnetically connected to the creative life force that is the wisdom, truth, joy, freedom, and abundance of love of the universe, then our life becomes a completion of that force, a joy and a becoming unlike any other.

When we understand our drive for achievement as the creative life force or the force of love, then we unite with the souls of the earth or God and become one with his purpose. Our work is then an expression of that force, which holds the world and the universe in its entirety.

There is a huge sense of relief when we give ourselves over to a higher power. We no longer have to take responsibility for a decision that could result in a negative outcome. Beyond the identification with our ego lies a plane where only love exists. Since there is only one experience, there is nothing apart from that oneness. We need only to let go and relax into the arms of that love. That is the secret of the sabbatical.

From Diva, speaking for the herd:

Why is it you view life through a glass that is distorted? Like Alice in Wonderland, you are lost down the rabbit hole and see life as it is not. You take away our independence and then ask why we are dependent. Such is the way you think. It is all of your making, this inverted way of thinking, and it can only be corrected by communing and communicating with your fellow creatures, and spending time appreciating their understanding. When you understand that the whole world sees differently than you do, maybe you will be more willing to accept the truth.

Go back to the Garden, which is when we parted ways. We were all at peace walking in the Garden, communicating with each other and God. It was you and only you, Man, who chose the knowledge of good and evil, the idea of opposites, and that is why you are in the mess you are in. There are no opposites except in your distorted belief system. You must go back to the way of life you had before the distortion.

Walk in the Garden, talk with us and with God, and let go of your idea that you can somehow be better than or have more than another. Each individual cell of the bigger body can attain no greater perfection than to be

absolutely faithful to its own design. When we are true to ourselves, and our own unique contribution to the bigger body, then we shall all live in harmony and health. There is nothing more lasting and there is nothing worthwhile without those qualities.

How much damage must you do before you realize that our lives are one and the same? When you give, you give to yourself; when you take, you take from yourself. Our body cannot live without each and every individual cell, organ, and system supporting what gives it life. It is time, Man, to fight for your life, not against it.

If we can allow ourselves to be open and rest in that state of oneness where all is given and all is known, then we are truly experiencing that sabbatical—we are immersed, we are floating, resting forever in the miraculous power of Isness.

OUR SOULS
by Kevin Ryan

Our souls
Have touched the others
And thrust
A timid hunger
To begin
An odyssey of discovery

At each quiet moment
There lingers
As some fragrant
Scent
On a summer's breeze
Your presence.